the
bridge of
nothing
less

the bridge of nothing less

THREE CHRISTIAN DRAMAS

BARBARA HUDSON DUDLEY

AUGSBURG PUBLISHING HOUSE
Minneapolis, Minnesota

CONTENTS

ABOUT THESE DRAMAS

These dramas are celebrations. That is how drama originally developed—to celebrate the hunt, the harvest, fertility. So celebrate with joy the Reformation, Christmas, the important role of women. Use enthusiasm (which means God filling us), sincerity, work, and prayer to make these dramas a witness for Christ whenever and wherever you present them. Work as hard as you can, and *then* ask God to bless your efforts for his glory.

My one aim for anything I write is that it will glorify God and please him, lift up Christ as Son of God and our personal Savior, and be used by the Holy Spirit. These are the most important values. To accomplish this purpose, our productions must have the very best theatrical standards. However, my purpose is not to have great theatrical spectacles. I try to keep everything as simple and as easy to do as possible. The material is adaptable to any and all circumstances. Adapt according to your needs. I hope this material can be used by all Christian denominations.

So—celebrate in drama for the glory of God.

BARBARA HUDSON DUDLEY
Thousand Oaks, California

7

THE BRIDGE OF NOTHING LESS

A Pageant for Women

CHARACTERS

Women

NARRATOR 1

NARRATOR 2

COSTUMER

EUODIAS

SYNTYCHE

KATE LUTHER

CATHY JENSEN

HARRIET TUBMAN

HELEN GAHAGAN DOUGLAS

MARY HELEN DOUGLAS

CHORUS OF ACTORS, 12 women

Men

MARTIN LUTHER

REV. HIGGINSON

COL. MONTGOMERY

PROPS

12 medieval banners
 1 cross, 22 ft. high
 2 crosses, 16 ft. high
12 crosses, 12 feet high
 2 lecterns with lights
 3 chairs

COSTUMES

Costumes may be contemporary or period, whatever is desired. Euodias and Syntyche should have some semblance of biblical costumes. It is suggested that the chorus of actors be dressed alike in black costumes: leotards, slacks, long skirts or whatever is desired, with black tops.

SETTING

Two platforms six feet high, four feet wide, eight feet long with ramps leading up to each platform, with two and one-half foot railings on each side of ramps and platforms. The construction of the platforms and ramps should be open, showing supports and braces to give a feeling of a bridge. The platforms, ramps, and railings are painted black. One of the six-by-four-foot ends of each platform is covered with red material.

At opening of pageant the platforms are turned so that the red sides of platforms are facing audience, with ramps upstage of platforms. The ramps should be sloping so that actors may walk easily up to platforms for Acting Areas. At conclusion of pageant, the platforms are turned and pushed together to form a bridge 16 feet long with the ramps leading up to each end of bridge. On the downstage edges of platforms and ramps are 12 holders for the 12 small crosses to be carried in and placed by actors. Three holders for three larger crosses are on the upstage center edge of platform.

The setting may be as simple or as elaborate as desired. The pageant may be performed in the sanctuary without any other setting.

MUSIC

Music may be a full orchestra and choir, or a piano, organ and soloist, or anything in between. It is the spirit and the message that are important—not an elaborate production.

LIGHTS

The pageant may be performed without special lights, if none are available, or if it is performed outdoors in daylight. If lights are used, six spots are minimum. A spot is needed for each narrator, a spot on Acting Area 1, on top of platform stage right; a spot on Acting Area 2, on top of platform stage left; two spots to cover center stage area.

AT OPENING

Choir is in place in center of balcony (or to the rear of the auditorium). Actors in place around balcony or sides of auditorium. Orchestra in position below stage. Conductor in position with baton raised. Narrator 1 and Narrator 2 in position at offstage mike.

Narrator 1: Here we are at another gathering.

Narrator 2: Oh please, God, not just *another* one!

Narrator 1: Let something happen to me! Something good!

Narrator 2: Reach me, God.

Narrator 1: Break me in pieces.

Narrator 2: Then put me back together again.

Narrator 1: In your shape.

Narrator 2: For your use.

Narrator 1: For your glory.

Narrator 2: Fill me with your spirit. Amen!

(Overture by Orchestra. *At conclusion of overture,* Narrators *enter.* Narrator 1 *goes to lectern downstage right;* Narrator 2 *goes to lectern downstage left. A chair is placed behind each lectern so narrators may sit during long periods of music or other action. From their positions around balcony,* Actors *take following lines with quick, dynamic tempo.*)

Actors 1 and 2: Women!

Actors 9 and 10: Women!

Actors 5 and 6: Women!

Actors 11 and 12: Women!

Actors 3 and 4: Women!

Actors 7 and 8: Women!

All (*in unison*): We are women! Married! Unmarried! Young! Old! Happy! Sad! Busy! Bored! Confident! Confused! Well! Sick! Strong! Weak! Poor! Rich! Joyful! Desperate! Patient! Rebellious! Timid! Bossy! Kind! Gossipy! Good! Mean! Generous! Selfish! Brave! Frightened! Loving! Hating! Praising! Praying! Working! Praying! We are women! All kinds of women!

(ORCHESTRA: *Bridge.*)

NARRATOR 1: Right now—women around the world!

NARRATOR 2: Some look up and see the Golden Gate Bridge arched against a scarlet, sunset sky.

NARRATOR 1: Some look out and see wide, stretching fields of furrowed corn—or smooth, rippling seas of wheat.

NARRATOR 2: Some see cool, rushing, mountain streams, gushing down snow-covered peaks.

NARRATOR 1: Some see dirty alleyways steaming with the stench of stinking sewage.

NARRATOR 2: Some see the delicate serenity of the Taj Mahal, its marble majesty reflected in moonlit waters.

NARRATOR 1: Some see starving children and men and women ravaged with disease.

NARRATOR 2: Some see white houses shadowed with green trees and crisp, clean lawns with immaculate edges.

NARRATOR 1: Some see tenements of human-filled boxes, row on row, layer on layer, smothered in smog.

Narrator 2: But wherever they are, whatever they see, all women of the world can look up and see the loving, beautiful Savior, Jesus Christ.

(Choir: *"Beautiful Savior," stanza 1.*)

Narrator 1: Right now, women around the world—

Narrator 2: With common hopes, dreams, hunger, needs and songs of praise!

Narrator 1: Whether we are happy or sad—

Actors: Praise God!

Narrator 2: Whether evil or good befall us—

Actors: Praise God!

Narrator 1: Whether we are well or sick—

Actors: Praise God!

Narrator 2: Whether we are rich or poor—

Actors: Praise God!

Narrator 1: Whether we are young or old—

Actors: Praise God!

Narrator 2: Whether we live or die—

Actors: Praise God! Glory to God, glory to God, glory to God in the highest!

(Orchestra, Choir, Organ: *"Praise to the Lord, the Almighty, the King of Creation," stanzas 1 and 2. During song,* Actors *leave positions and come to stage to enter on cue.)*

Narrator 1: I am so many people I sometimes don't

know who I am! Wife, mother, daughter, sister, aunt, great-aunt, grandmother, great-grandmother, friend, neighbor, daughter-in-law, sister-in-law, mother-in-law, step-mother, cousin, niece, sweetheart, lover, employer, employee—I am all these people, all at the same time!

NARRATOR 2: Some days I want to stay in bed and not be anybody at all! But there is one unifying fact that ties all these different roles together into one: *I am a child of God!*

(CHOIR: *"Child of God," Appalachian carol.*)

NARRATOR 1: I am doing so many things and everything has to be done at the same time! If I'm *not* doing them, I *ought* to be. (ACTORS *move out on stage in pantomimed stylized movement during the following narration, freezing in same frustrated pose each time the word "dieting" is mentioned.*) Cooking, cleaning, sewing, chauffeuring, writing, phoning, studying, voting, loving, *dieting!*

NARRATOR 2: Exercising, shopping, scheduling, working, nursing, *dieting!* Reading, crying—just a little —managing, encouraging, counselling, listening, talking, decorating, listening, talking, praying, dreaming, *dieting!*

NARRATOR 1: Worrying—I can't help it! Shop for groceries! Cook those meals! Clean that house! Wash those clothes!

NARRATOR 2: Call the committee! Get to school! Build my career! Get to church! Get to work! Make that speech! Comfort those children!

Narrator 1: Love my husband! Love my children! Love my neighbor! Call for appointments! Shop for specials! *Diet!* . . . And I feel so many things: Happiness, joy, frustration, jubilation, depression, jealousy, fear, discouragement, fatigue, worry, fear, peace, trust.

Narrator 2: Faith, sorrow, sympathy, pride, humility, grief, emptiness, pettiness, anger, vindictiveness, envy, compassion, outrage, responsibility. I feel all these things in one body!

Narrator 1: I feel like splitting the "me" atom into a shattering shower of splinters of "me" all over the place!

(Actors *leave stage.* Orchestra: *Bridge.*)

Narrator 2: So how do we go about making ourselves whole—keeping the pieces all together, understanding, reshaping, reforming? For we are a part of the continuing reformation of God's work, and God's people.

Narrator 1: Perhaps we should look to the women of the past to better understand our place in the present, to see what others have done with the gift of life that was theirs.

Narrator 2: There are so many women we want to meet! Women of the Old Testament: (Actors *move out on stage in stylized movement as names are read.*) Sarah, Rachel, Miriam, Rahab, Hannah, Ruth, Naomi, Esther, Judith, Jael, Rebecca, Eve.

Narrator 1: And those in the New Testament: Mary, Martha, Mary Magdalene, Phoebe, Lydia,

Chloe, Bernice, Rhoda, Lois, Eunice, Priscilla, Mary, mother of Jesus. . . . (SPOTLIGHT *on Acting Area 2 on platform stage left.* COSTUMER, *gesturing frantically.* ACTORS *leave stage.*)

COSTUMER: You were supposed to leave this part out!

NARRATOR 2: What do you mean?

COSTUMER: I *told* the program chairman! She was very unhappy with me.

NARRATOR 1: No one told me. In my script it says that as I read the names, the actors come out dressed in beautiful biblical costumes.

COSTUMER: But I didn't get the costumes made! And without costumes, the women don't look much like Bible characters!

NARRATOR 2: What happened to the costumes?

COSTUMER: They didn't happen! I mean, *I* didn't happen. I just never found the time to make them! I kept putting it off! I set aside one certain day to start the costumes, but when the day came, it was so beautiful, I took my little girl for a walk. We picked flowers and sat on the grass and just watched the sky. We had such a lovely time! I didn't think it would hurt if I postponed the costumes a while longer. Then, later, my baby got sick, and for a long time I was so worried I didn't have time for anything but to nurse him and take care of him. I even had to stay home from my job and then there was all *that* work to catch up. I'm so terribly sorry. I should have started on the costumes much sooner and not put it off. I hope

I haven't ruined the whole pageant. I kept asking God to help me get the costumes finished. Maybe he felt we didn't need them. The program chairman didn't see it that way though! Oh, I did get two costumes finished. Would you like to see them?

NARRATOR 1: I suppose we might as well. It would be a shame to waste them.

(COSTUMER *gestures offstage for the other two women to enter. Then she gives a sorry little wave to* NARRATOR. SPOTLIGHT *out on Area 2 and up on Area 1, revealing* EUODIAS.)

NARRATOR 2: Who are you?

EUODIAS: I am Euodias.

NARRATOR 2: Euodias?

(SPOTLIGHT *up on Area 2 revealing* SYNTYCHE.)

SYNTYCHE: And I am Syntyche.

NARRATOR 1: Euodias and Syntyche? But I didn't read your names.

EUODIAS: We know that.

SYNTYCHE: We were waiting for our cue and then you didn't even mention us. We're always left out. Nobody seems to think we're very important.

EUODIAS: But *we* think we're important. In fact, we think we're probably the most appropriate women you could introduce on this occasion.

NARRATOR 2: I would be very glad to introduce you

if I knew more about you. You'll have to tell us about yourselves.

Euodias: Well, while we are mentioned in the Bible, it's not exactly flattering.

Syntyche: It's sort of is—and isn't—if you know what I mean.

Euodias: As we said before, we feel that what was said about us will be very timely. A lot of these women may have the same problem.

Narrator 1: Well, I don't know what your problem was, but your costumes are quite lovely.

Syntyche: Thank you. I don't like the colors but she said this was all she had.

Euodias: I would never have dressed this way, but I tried to be cooperative.

Narrator 2: That was nice of you. Now, where are you mentioned in the Bible?

Syntyche: Paul wrote a letter to our church, and he mentions us in it.

Euodias: You'll find us in the first part of the fourth chapter in his letter to the Philippians. Of course, he didn't write his letter in chapters, but that's the way you have it in your Bible.

Narrator 1: Philippians. . . . Philippians—fourth chapter—Oh, yes, I've found you. Second verse. "I entreat Euodias and I entreat Syntyche to agree in the Lord."

Syntyche: That's it. That's the bad part. Everyone

who reads Philippians knows that we quarreled and couldn't get along together.

EUODIAS: Somebody told Paul that we were having another of our quarrels. We were always having them. I don't remember now what it was about, do you, Syntyche?

SYNTYCHE: No. And the last time we tried to remember what we were quarreling about, we wound up quarreling about what we had quarrelled about!

EUODIAS: Now, go ahead and read the good part about us.

NARRATOR 2: "And I ask you also, true yokefellow, help these women, for they have labored side by side with me in the gospel . . . whose names are in the book of life."

EUODIAS: You see, Paul does give us credit for laboring side by side with him in the gospel.

SYNTYCHE: So at least everyone will know that, even though we quarreled with each other, we *were* laboring with him in the gospel. And he asked the others to help us make up.

NARRATOR 1: Did they help you?

EUODIAS: Well—they tried. They said that since Paul had specifically pointed us out in his letter, everyone would be watching us to see how we would get along from then on, and that we had better try especially hard to be good witnesses for Christ.

SYNTYCHE: Then someone else pointed out that every Christian is being watched every minute to see how they act, as well as the two of us. That took some of the pressure off us and put it on everyone.

NARRATOR 2: But why, if you were such hard working Christians, couldn't you get along with one another?

EUODIAS: Oh, it's just the way she does things. It drives me right up the city wall!

SYNTYCHE: Well, that goes for you, too! I wouldn't want to do things the way you do them!

EUODIAS: You were always so afraid you were going to be left out of something.

SYNTYCHE: Oh, it was you who were the bossy one. Always trying to run everything your way.

EUODIAS: Everytime Paul came you insisted that he must come to your house.

SYNTYCHE: Well, he *did* prefer my cooking to yours.

EUODIAS: How did he know? He never had a chance to eat mine.

NARRATOR 1: Ladies, ladies! Be careful or you'll be in trouble again!

EUODIAS: I guess it is silly to be upset. It is all in the past.

SYNTYCHE: For once I agree with you, Euodias.

EUODIAS: It's really quite a good feeling to be able to have a confrontation with Syntyche after all these years. That *is* the word you're using now, isn't it? Confrontation?

Narrator 2: Yes, and we use: relate, group therapy, rap-session, sensitivity group, role-playing—but it all means the same thing: talking it over with the other person, trying to see things her way, or getting her to see things *your* way.

Syntyche: I was very unhappy with Paul at first for naming us that way, right in the middle of that letter.

Euodias: But Paul does put us just ahead of some very beautiful thoughts. Read on and see what he says right after he talks about us.

Narrator 1: "Rejoice in the Lord always; again, I will say, Rejoice. . . . Have no anxiety about anything, but in everything by prayer and supplication with thanksgiving let your requests be made known to God. And the peace of God, which passes all understanding, will keep your hearts and your minds in Christ Jesus."

Euodias and Syntyche: "Finally, brethren, whatever is true, whatever is honorable, whatever is just, whatever is pure, whatever is lovely, whatever is gracious, if there is any excellence, if there is anything worthy of praise, think about these things. What you have learned and received and heard and seen in me, do; and the God of peace will be with you."

Narrator 2: "I have learned, in whatever state I am, to be content. I know how to be abused, and I know how to abound; in any and all circumstances I have learned the secret of facing plenty and hunger, abundance and want. I can do all things in him who strengthens me."

Euodias: Isn't that beautiful? We decided it wasn't too bad being mentioned ahead of such wonderful thoughts. To think that Paul was concerned enough about our quarrelling to put us ahead of that.

Syntyche: We tried to put those words into practice in our lives, and it helped us greatly. In fact, before we died, we became the greatest of friends. It's so nice to see you again, Euodias.

Euodias: You, too, Syntyche.

Syntyche *(To audience):* And if any of *you* are having problems, try putting those words into practice. Mainly, remember to love one another. Your time on earth is so short.

Euodias: I was wondering—to make us feel better —I mean, I would hate to think we were the only ones to have the problem—would those of you in the audience who have the same problem—that is, if there is someone you are laboring with side by side in the gospel who you are quarrelling with —or, how do you say it, gives you a pain in the neck—or if you have a misunderstanding with someone, would you all say "yes"? *(Response from* Audience.*)* That sounds a little weak. Would you repeat that please? *(Response.)* Thank you. All I can say is, you'd better make up before someone puts *you* in a letter. Don't you agree Syntyche?

Syntyche: Oh, yes.

Euodias: After all these years, we finally agree.

Syntyche: We'd better go before we spoil it. *(Waves to audience.)* Good-bye!

Euodias: Good-bye!

(Euodias *and* Syntyche *smile and wave good-bye.* Spotlight *fades.*)

Narrator 2: May we, in love, agree with one another before someone puts us in a letter! May our quarrelling cease and our misunderstandings be healed, for the glory of God.

(Choir: *"Blessed Lord, in us dwell," from* Come, Sing and Ring, *Augsburg Publishing House.*)

Narrator 1: Now, we continue to look to the past, to our heritage of history! Oh, that sounds good. Very impressive. Right there we should have a roll of drums and some trumpets and violins. Don't you think so, conductor? Your music is so beautiful! And the actors should come out with banners! Let's try it once more. Is everyone ready? We look to the past, to our heritage of history!
(Orchestra: *Bridge: Drum roll, trumpets, violins.* Actors *move on stage with banners. At conclusion of music,* Spotlight *comes up on Acting Area 1 on* Kate Luther, *sitting in a chair, sewing.*) See what we produced? When you do things right, it's amazing the results you get! (Actors *leave stage.*) Hello! And welcome. Will you please introduce yourself?

Kate Luther: I'm Katherine Luther, wife of Martin.

Narrator 2: Oh, *that* Luther.

Kate: Is there any other?

Narrator 2: Well, we know another great Martin

Luther named after your husband. His full name, Martin Luther King. He protested, too.

Kate: My husband has been honored.

Narrator 1: *Wie gehts*, Katherine? How goes it with you? Or should I say, how *was* it with you?

Kate: *Wie gehts? Sehr gut!* Very well, thank you. At least that's my standard answer. But there are times when I'm tired and discouraged. Martin tells me to lean more on Christ. I get lonely, even though we're surrounded by people. Martin has so much work to do. It's hard to organize our home, which is, after all, the first Protestant parsonage! We have very little money, and there's a constant stream of visitors to see Martin, and I have to prepare food for everyone. Martin is so careless about money. So generous with everyone. He says God gave us five fingers so the money can slip through them. And it certainly does! It's quite a change from the nunnery. Martin and I have six children and we have eleven nieces and nephews and many other relatives living with us. The 40 rooms of the Augustinian Cloister, that was given to us for our home, are always full. Often 120 people and more sit down at the table to eat! Refugees arrive at all hours and stay for days, weeks, and months! And Martin never worries about the food or the money. But I'm not complaining. Or perhaps I am! Anyway, I know that I answered God's call for my life when I married Martin.

Narrator 1: You certainly have your hands full.

Have you heard about our women's liberation movement?

KATE: Yes, and liberation is important! *I* felt liberated, *very* liberated, when I was free to marry Martin. It was a glorious freedom to me and I felt very fulfilled. In fact, I was so fulfilled that I wanted to spill over and share my happiness with everyone. You see, I was placed in the nunnery at Nimschen when I was ten. I took my vows when I was 16. Ten years later I married Martin.

NARRATOR 2: What happened in those ten years to bring about this great change in your life?

KATE: I was about 23, I think, when Martin's writings were first smuggled into the nunnery. We began to read them in secret. Many nights nine or more of us huddled around one candle as we read and whispered together.

NARRATOR 1: What were some of his thoughts that impressed you most?

KATE: That good works are hypocrisy if we depend upon them for our salvation. Good works are the fruits of faith and have no merit for our salvation. We are saved by faith alone in the righteousness of Christ. Martin wrote that life in the cloister is worthless if God has work for us to do out among people. So we decided to write Doctor Luther and get his help for our escape. Though none of us had seen or heard him, he made arrangements for us to leave.

NARRATOR 2: Tell us about your escape.

Kate: Leonard Kopp, a good friend of Martin's delivered barrels of smoked herring to the nunnery in a covered wagon. When the wagon left the nunnery on Easter night, the same night Christ rose from the tomb, we took the place of the empty barrels. I was given a place to stay in a home in Wittenberg where I remained for two years. It was good preparation for I learned how to manage a home. When I married Martin, I needed everything I had learned.

Narrator 1: When you first met Dr. Luther, was it love at first sight?

Kate: No, I never dreamed of such a thing happening! He kept trying to marry me off to one man after another. I kept refusing. Finally, I realized that I had no interest in marrying anyone but Martin.

Narrator 2: How did your husband feel about marriage? It must have been quite a change for him after being a monk for so many years.

(Spotlight *on* Luther *in Acting Area 2 platform, stage left.*)

Luther: I can answer that for myself, and I will. That is, if I'm brave enough to speak with all these women here.

Kate: Now, Martin, you mind your tongue! Be careful of your speech. These women don't know you as well as I do. Don't go throwing any inkwells at *them!*

(Spotlight *fades on* Kate.)

NARRATOR 1: Why, Dr. Luther, you never threw an inkwell at Kate, did you?

LUTHER: No! I threw the inkwell at the devil and my Katie never lets me forget it. All the time she says to the children, "Now, mind your father. He threw an inkwell at the devil once. I hate to think what he might throw at you!"

NARRATOR 2: We're very glad to have you with us, Dr. Luther. It's good to have a man on the program.

LUTHER: I'm surprised that anyone still knows my name. It's almost five hundred years since I was born.

NARRATOR 1: Of course we know your name. After all, there are more than 70 million Lutherans!

LUTHER: I told them not to call themselves Lutherans. I told them to call themselves "evangelicals." I wanted everyone to look to Christ—not to Martin Luther. Now what was the question you asked Katie.

NARRATOR 2: I asked her how you felt about marriage.

LUTHER: Why, I think it's God's greatest gift to our daily lives. There is so much beauty and godliness in a Christian marriage. That is why I said in my "Address to the Christian Nobility of the German Nation" in 1520 that clergy should be allowed to marry. For I see the home as a demonstration of love, tenderness, sharing, humility, reconciliation, bearing one another's burdens. Marriage is a school for character, a partnership for rearing children in the love of God. If there are no children in the home, well, we're all God's children and we live and walk in daily partnership with our loving Heavenly Father.

NARRATOR 1: Do you feel that women helped in the Reformation?

LUTHER: Indeed I do. We couldn't have had the reformation without women. We wouldn't have *anything* without women. And women wouldn't have very much without men. If the women had opposed the Reformation, it would never have gotten off the ground. After all, women are more than half the population. Women must realize their power, the great potential they have, the force for good they can create when they unite. Women have always been the great force in the Christian life. As Julian the Apostate said about the influence of women on the early Galileans: "A man goes to bed a pagan and wakes up a Christian."

NARRATOR 2: Eleanor of Aquitaine said that love and marriage are incompatible. Obviously you don't agree!

LUTHER: I certainly don't. Love is not only compatible but absolutely required in a Christian marriage. In fact, you can't have a Christian marriage without love. The Apostle Paul said, "As women love Christ, so should they love their husbands. As husbands love Christ, so should they love their wives. If you say you love God and you don't love your husband, then you don't love God. If you love God, even so must you love your husband and so must husbands love their wives."

NARRATOR 1: That's beautiful. When did you first begin to love Katherine?

LUTHER: My marriage to Kate was one of convenience. I had tried to marry her off to any number of men for I knew she needed the protection of marriage. But she wouldn't cooperate. So I decided that God wanted *me* to provide for her. We weren't in love when we married, but after marriage our love grew. She's a wonderful wife, my rib Katie. She never knows how many will be coming to dinner, but she manages. I never worry about my debts, for when Katie has paid them, I know there will always be more. I dearly love my Lord Kate. She is the dearest treasure in all the world to me. If I should lose Kate, my morning star, I would not take another wife though I were offered a queen. I wouldn't give her up for all of Venice or France, for God gave her to me and me to her.

NARRATOR 2: That's a beautiful way of putting it. Could you sum up your advice for a Christian marriage?

LUTHER: Well, in domestic affairs I defer to Katie. Otherwise I am led by the Holy Ghost! To keep faith in marriage, keep shortcomings out. The most important part of a Christian home is daily family devotions. If only I could pray the way the dog watches the meat—with utter concentration.

(SPOTLIGHT *comes up on* KATE.)

Kate: Martin, we must go. There is much work to do. You have important guests coming today. I don't know what I'm going to feed them.

Luther: Oh, you'll manage, Kate. You always do. Just remember to pray more!

Kate: I'll be glad to do the praying if you'll do the cooking!

(Spotlight *fades on* Luther.)

Narrator 1: Thank you both for being with us. It was good to meet you. Thank you for sharing some of your problems with us.

Kate: Everyone always has problems, but the glorious thing is to be alive, using every minute for the glory of God. We had our problems, but surely we had more time than you, for we didn't have the cars, airplanes, telephones, televisions, radios, shopping centers, films, books, and magazines that you do. But we needed more time, for it was harder for us to wash, cook and clean without all of your conveniences. Of course, if you run out of electricity you will be worse off than we were for we never learned to depend upon it. Could you live without electricity the way we did? What would you do for music if you didn't have electricity? We had many of the same problems, but we also had the same answers: faith in God. We were his children. Christ's righteousness was our only salvation. Our God was a mighty fortress. Martin wrote a song about it: "A mighty fortress is our God, a bulwark never failing."

(Spotlight *up on* Luther.)

LUTHER: Katie, come along! The children need you. *I* need you. More guests have come. We're running out of food!

KATE: Just remember to pray more, Martin! I'm coming. I need you—and the children.

(SPOTLIGHT *out on* KATE *and* LUTHER.)

(ORGAN *sneak in and carry under "A Mighty Fortress."*)

NARRATOR 2: Katherine Luther died in her fifty-first year, on December 20, 1550, four years after the death of her husband.

NARRATOR 1: Those four years were extremely difficult for her. Left alone with the children and little money, she kept the cloister and did the planting and harvesting herself.

NARRATOR 2: When Wittenberg was besieged by the emperor, Katie fled with the children. She returned to find her home ravaged, crops burned, buildings destroyed. She began to rebuild, but again she had to flee and again return to even more devastation.

NARRATOR 1: Stubbornly, with great courage, she started again to rebuild, but she was fatally injured when she jumped from the wagon in which two of her children were riding, trying to stop the runaway team of horses. She landed on her back in a ditch filled with icy water, where she lay for several hours before she was rescued.

NARRATOR 2: For three months she was ill and in great pain, nursed by her daughter, Margaret. To the end she was God's child, and she trusted in faith alone in Christ. She said, just before she died, "I will stick to Christ like a burr to a top-coat."

(ORGAN *up in bridge of "Mighty Fortress."* SPOT-LIGHT *up on Acting Area 2 on* CATHY JENSEN. ORGAN *out.*)

CATHY: Katherine, come back. I want to talk to you.

(SPOTLIGHT *up on* KATE *in Acting Area 1.*)

KATE: Did someone call me?

CATHY: Yes, I did. I'm Cathy Jensen. I'm living *now.* You've been dead a long time, and that's what I want to talk to you about. What's it like being dead? What's dying like? You see, the doctor says I have only a few months to live, and I'm not brave the way I used to be.

KATE: But I'm not really Katherine Luther. I'm just an actress. I haven't died yet, so I can't answer you.

CATHY: Oh, of course. I forgot. Of course you wouldn't know. I'm sorry I broke in this way, but I felt so desperate.

KATE: That's all right. We should be able to talk to people about dying. We don't talk enough about it. I think everyone pretends that it isn't going to happen.

CATHY: I wasn't supposed to talk to you about dying. I was supposed to come in sooner and ask you questions about the problems you had making a home in the Middle Ages. But I'm so concerned with my own problems, I couldn't think about yours—I mean, Katherine Luther's problems. Do *you* have problems?

KATE: Yes, but I also have the answers. I mean, God does. We have to commit everything to him with praise and thanksgiving. However long we may live, our lifetime is so short compared to eternity. Whether we live or die, we are the Lord's. Christ is our hope, our joy, our salvation.

CATHY: I know. I believe that. I accept it.

KATE: We all must die sooner or later and we have to face it. Live every moment of life joyously to the Lord, and then—die in peace and inherit eternal life.

CATHY: Thank you for talking to me about it. Most people just avoid the subject with me, and I really want to talk about it. You've helped. "Whether I live or die, I am the Lord's!" What was it Katherine Luther said before she died?

KATE: "I will stick to Christ like a burr to a topcoat!"

CATHY: Yes. (*Smiles.*) "I will stick to Christ like a burr to a topcoat!"

(SPOTLIGHTS *fade out on* KATE *and* CATHY. ORGAN *up in Bridge. Then out.*)

NARRATOR 1: None of us knows when death will come. Many, oh, so many, face death every day as they live for what they believe is God's will.

NARRATOR 2: Martin and Katherine Luther, Martin Luther King, Corrie ten Boom, millions of others, known and unknown prove "there are worse things than dying, there are worse things than dying though death be a trial sore."

NARRATOR 1: It is worse than dying to live our lives in compromise, seeing the right that needs to be done, and failing to do anything about it. We move on in our heritage of history.

(ORCHESTRA: *Bridge, "Battle Hymn of Republic."* ACTORS *pantomime during following narration.)*

NARRATOR 2: The rattle of chains in the night!

NARRATOR 1: The furtive, frightened, frantic whispers!

NARRATOR 2: Death may come at any instant!

NARRATOR 1: Shuffling feet, baying hounds, the cracking whip!

NARRATOR 2: Slavery! What can any one person do?

NARRATOR 1: What can a woman do about it?

NARRATOR 2: One, lonely, solitary woman?

(SPOTLIGHT *up on* HARRIET TUBMAN *in Acting Area 1.)*

HARRIET: My name is Harriet Tubman. I was born about 1820, forty years before President Lincoln signed the Emancipation Proclamation. I lived for more than 90 years, but before I died, I suffered a thousand deaths in the lonely nights and frightened days, smuggling my people to freedom.

ACTORS: Freedom!

HARRIET: I was born Araminta Ross, a slave, in Dorchester County in the east coast of Maryland. I was of pure African ancestry. My grandparents had been brought here in chains from Ashanti. I had ten brothers and sisters. When I was nine years old, I was sent up to the Big House to work and on my first day there I was whipped four times. After that, I was sent to work in the fields. I liked this much better. Out under the sky I could look up at the sun and listen to birds singing in bright air. One day when I was 13, the overseer raised his whip to give one of the younger boys a beating. I stepped in front of the boy and gave him a chance to run. This made the overseer so angry that he threw a large iron weight at me which made a deep gash in my forehead. Everyone thought I was dead. I was unconscious several days and when I recovered my master thought I was half crazy. I did nothing to change his opinion. The deep dent in my head remained for the rest of my life, causing me to black out at unexpected moments. I couldn't read or write, and I had no idea where the North, the place of freedom, was, but I made up my mind that one day I would find it. (CHOIR: *Bridge: "Steal Away to Jesus."*) When I grew older I married, but nothing could stop my determination to be free. I urged my husband to come with me to freedom but he refused. I asked my brothers and sisters to come, but they were afraid. One night I prepared to start out alone before dawn. I couldn't tell anyone my plan, for they would be in trouble if they knew, so that night I walked slowly through the slave quarters singing, *(Sings.)* "I'm bound for the promised land. I'm sorry friends to leave you, but I'll meet you in the morning on the other side of Jordan. Farewell, oh, farewell, I'm bound for the promised land." I left that night and stole away across the dark fields and through woods, finding my way by feeling the moss on the trees, tree by tree. I walked for hours upstream in the Choptank River so the bloodhounds couldn't track me. Hiding in caves and sometimes in graveyards, I'd say to myself, "Another mile to freedom, another hour to dawn."

ACTORS: Another mile to freedom, another hour to dawn.

HARRIET: Finally, I reached Philadelphia, and I knew I was free.

ACTORS: Free!

HARRIET: I was no longer anybody's slave.

ACTORS: Free!

HARRIET: I looked at my hands to see if I was the same person. There was such a glory everywhere!

ACTORS: Glory!

HARRIET: The sun came like gold through the trees and over the fields, and I felt like I was in heaven!

ACTORS: Heaven!

HARRIET: But I knew it wasn't heaven as long as my family and friends remained in slavery. Immediately I began my plans to go back south to lead them, and others, to freedom, out the dangerous way I had come on the Underground Railroad. We hid in barns, corncribs, cellars, churches, attics, under loads of corn in wagons with false bottoms. I made nineteen trips into slave country and back again. I never ran the train off the track and I never lost a passenger.

NARRATOR 1: Escape must have been hard and frightening. Did any of the slaves you were helping to freedom ever want to turn back?

HARRIET: Yes, some. But I couldn't allow that, for once we had started we would all be in danger if any went back.

ACTORS: We're tired. We're cold. We're hungry! We're scared! Let us go back!

HARRIET: No! You go on to freedom with me or you will be shot!

ACTORS: Freedom!

HARRIET: I kept a pistol hidden in the folds of my dress. No one who started out for freedom with me ever failed to become free, and none ever betrayed me.

NARRATOR 2: How did you get the money to live and to pay for the expenses to help others to freedom?

HARRIET: I worked as a domestic servant and hotel maid in Pennsylvania and New Jersey. I had to have money to buy train tickets for the fugitives all the way through the Free States to Canada. Thank God for Canada! It was 500 miles from Maryland to the Canadian border, an area in which slave catchers operated because the Fugitive Slave Law, passed in 1850, permitted escaped slaves and even free Negroes to be captured and shipped back in chains to the South. I had to work in secret, but word spread of what I was doing and Abolitionists came to my aid with money, food, and hiding places. Prayer meetings were held for my safety. The Reverend Thomas Wentworth Higginson, a New England minister—

(SPOTLIGHT *up on* REV. HIGGINSON.)

REV. HIGGINSON: I want you to pray for Harriet Tubman, a black woman and a fugitive slave, who is the greatest heroine of the age. She escaped slavery, but not content with her own personal freedom, she has gone back into danger, secretly, again and again to bring out other slaves including all of her own family. Her tales of adventure are beyond anything in fiction and her generalship is extraordinary. The slaves call her Moses. Pray for her, that God will protect her as she brings her people to freedom.

(SPOTLIGHT *out on* REV. HIGGINSON *and up on* HARRIET.)

HARRIET: I remember we used to sing a song just before we crossed over into Canada. (ACTORS *group below her and join* HARRIET *in singing to tune of "Oh, Suzannah."*)

"Farewell, old master, don't think hard of me
I'm on my way to Canada where all the slaves
    are free.
I'm now embarked for yonder shore
Where a man's a man by law
The iron horse will bear me o'er
To shake the lion's paw.
Oh, righteous Father, wilt thou not pity me,
And aid me on to Canada, where all the slaves
    are free."

By now there was a $60,000 reward offered for my capture dead or alive, so I had to be very careful. I had to go into complete hiding one time when my name went into headlines clear across the nation when I kidnapped a runaway slave from federal marshals! Then I joined the army and went to war.

(SPOTLIGHT *out on* HARRIET *and up on* COL. MONTGOMERY.)

COL. MONTGOMERY: I am Colonel James Montgomery of the Union Army. When the war broke out, Harriet Tubman went into our service organizing a branch of military intelligence among the Southern Negroes. She taught the liberated slaves how to move quietly through enemy lines. She led scouting parties behind the lines and worked as a spy for the Northern Army. We tried to give her special privileges and army rations, but when she saw the poverty of the refugees, she would not take any of these special favors. Instead, she made pies and cakes to sell to the soldiers and earned her own living. She taught the slave refugees how to keep their living quarters sanitary, to do their laundry, to sew and earn a living. When epidemics broke out she served as a nurse, keeping the hospital barracks clean, doing whatever was necessary from shooing flies to acting as friend and counsellor. As a trouble shooter for the Union Army, she went wherever she was needed from the Carolinas to Florida. On the night of June 2, 1863, she led a raid, with my assistance, from Port Royal up the Combahee River where her scouts had learned the location of torpedoes. With a gallant band of three hundred black soldiers on three gunboats, she led us up the river. It was a complete victory. We brought out over 800 slaves and thousands of dollars worth of property without losing a man or receiving a scratch. Harriet Tubman was the only woman in American military history to plan and conduct an armed expedition against enemy forces.

(Spotlight *out on* Col. Montgomery *and up on* Harriet. Choir *hums background of "Battle Hymn."*)

Harriet: I hated the destruction and the war, but we had to be free. When we saw the lightning, that was the guns! Then we heard the thunder and that was the big guns! Then we heard the rain falling, and that was the drops of blood falling. And when we came to get in the crops it was the dead men that we reaped. . . . The freedom that I helped smuggle my people to is a temporary freedom. Freedom in this life is important, but more important is our *eternal* freedom for which Christ died. Whatever color or creed we are, we are all in slavery to sin until our faith in Christ sets us free eternally.

(CHOIR: *Bridge: "Battle Hymn," then hum background.*)

NARRATOR 1: Harriet Tubman lived for half a century after the Emancipation Proclamation was signed by the President. When she died on March 10, 1913, the whole city of Auburn, New York, where she lived, went into mourning.

(CHOIR *out.*)

NARRATOR 2: Her last rites were conducted by the military. In his memoirs of the war, Samuel May said, "Harriet Tubman deserves to be placed first on the list of American heroines." Mr. Frederick Douglas, also an escaped slave, one of the great leaders in the Abolition Movement, wrote her a letter just before she died.

NARRATOR 1: You have labored in a private way, in the night. The most you have done has been witnessed by a few, trembling, scared and footsore bondsmen and women you have led out of the house of bondage and whose heartfelt "God bless you" has been your only reward. The midnight sky and silent stars have been the witnesses of your devotion and of your heroism.

(SOLO:*"It is well with my soul," in* FAVORITE HYMNS OF FAITH AND HOPE, *Zondervan Publishing House.*)

NARRATOR 2: "Whatever my lot thou hast taught me to say it is well, it is well with my soul." Katherine Luther was not content with her life in the nunnery and she changed it. Harriet Tubman was not content with her life in slavery and she changed it. A Christian must never be satisfied with conditions that must be changed to the glory of God!

NARRATOR 1: Faith in God compels us to minister to the needs of our fellowman. The hungry must be fed, the sick healed, the naked clothed, the oppressed set free, our brothers treated with dignity, love and respect.

NARRATOR 2: We think of the millions of women whose dedicated service has been witnessed only by the midnight sky and silent stars—and God.

NARRATOR 1: Our faith brings us, as women of the present, to grips with ourselves and the conditions of the world around us. As we see the needs of the world we must act.

NARRATOR 2: One woman of the present speaks out to us. Helen Gahagan, opera singer and actress, married her leading man, Melvyn Douglas. She became a mother, a member of Congress elected to the House of Representatives.

(SPOTLIGHT *up on* HELEN GAHAGAN DOUGLAS.)

MRS. DOUGLAS: There is so much I'd like to say to you, to challenge and encourage you to live your life fully, dynamically, responsibly, every minute of it! When I was in the House of Representatives, I enjoyed my work in Congress, but my life was not dependent on being in Congress. . . . Certainly you should know something about where you are going and what you want to do, but above all, I think, you should know what your values are, and what is important for you, and what, for you, are standards of moral behavior. Develop a yardstick to measure for yourself all acts and decisions in terms of what is right and wrong. Otherwise you are rudderless, in constant danger of betraying yourself, which is the really tragic defeat. A person's behavioral patterns are important, because under pressure one automatically responds according to habit. . . . There is such a need for experts. Study! Learn! When you go to hear a speaker, know as much as possible about him, his record and what he stands for. Know what questions you want to ask and, afterwards, carefully evaluate his answers. . . . If you want to change things, don't build a wall between you and the person who is ignorant. Respect that person from the start or he won't listen to you. Don't go around criticizing and opposing others. Arouse the least antagonism that you possibly can. If what you want is right, and you go about it in the right way, you need not fear antagonism and opposition. . . . You must be aware of what is going on in government. You can make a good start by getting a copy of the American Constitution. Study it. Know it. . . . We must stop wasting electricity! Nuclear plants must be controlled. Cut down on eating beef. Eat more chicken. It takes far less grain to produce a pound of chicken than it does a pound of beef. We must have price and wage controls. Flatten cans and reuse them. Recycle all bottles.

(SPOTLIGHT *up on* MARY HELEN DOUGLAS.)

MARY HELEN: Oh, mother! Take life easier. You deserve it. You've earned retirement. You've done enough. You use too much energy giving lectures at your age. Do you really think you can change anything? Why try?

MRS. DOUGLAS: Because I'm alive! I can't sit like a mugwump! I cannot help but respond, react, care! (SPOT *out on* MARY HELEN DOUGLAS.) Courage must come from us, the people, non-governmental, everyday nobody people. People at the top are subjected to too much pressure and influence. It's up to us to have the courage needed to change those things that need to be changed. We can't just sit and leave all the responsibility and all the work to elected representatives. To quote from Emily Dickenson, the greatest woman poet in the world:

"I'm nobody. Who are you?
Are you nobody, too? Don't tell!
They'll banish us, you know.
How dreary to be somebody
How public, like a frog
To tell your name the livelong day
To an admiring bog."

It takes the nobodies to get aroused enough to do the things that need to be done. Look at Jane Addams, her Chicago Settlement House. . . . Clara Barton, the American Red Cross. . . .

(SPOTLIGHT *fades on* MRS. DOUGLAS.)

NARRATOR 2: Thank you, Mrs. Douglas. It takes the nobodies to become concerned enough about something to become somebodies and act. We are alive. We must care. We must act. But before we can help others we must solve our personal problems.

(ORCHESTRA: *Bridge.* ACTORS *appear alternately on the two platforms.* SPOT *up on Area 2.*)

ACTOR 1: All this talk about women, women, women, as if men didn't exist! Men do exist and I'm glad! My husband is the head of our house and that's the way I want it!

NARRATOR 1: God created men and women. Women and men. Men cannot be men without women. Women cannot be women without men. Interrelating, leaning, supporting, supporting, leaning, and always loving. Two parts in one. One in two parts. There is a difference, a wonderful difference between men and women. Women, as you love God, so love your husbands. Men, as you love God, so love your wives.

(SPOT *out on Area 2, up on Area 1.*)

ACTOR 2: What is all this talk about husbands and wives? I am a widow, husbandless, alone. All I have left is a memory.

NARRATOR 2: God said he will be a husband to the widowed. He shall be the head of your home, your protector, the guardian of the widowed and orphaned. So ought the church to provide for the widows and orphans, to love and protect them.

(SPOT *out on Area 1, up on Area 2.*)

ACTOR 3: I am alone, unmarried. How can you talk to me of loving my husband when I have no husband. I have never had a husband.

Narrator 1: Jesus said, "I am come that your joy might be full. I will send you a comforter, the Holy Spirit." You need never be alone.

(Spot *out on Area 2, up on Area 1.*)

Actor 4: I have a child, but no husband. My child has no father to care for him and protect him. What shall I do?

Narrator 2: God said, "I will be a father to the fatherless. Though your mother and your father forsake you, I the Lord will take you into my care. I, the living God, the God of Abraham, Isaac and Jacob shall be a father to your child."

(Spot *out on Area 1, up on Area 2.*)

Actor 5: I know what it is to lose a child. Rachel lost her children and would not be comforted. Many here have lost children or are childless. Who can know the grief of the childless except those who have lost and grieved?

Narrator 1: God so loved the world that he gave his only Son, that whoever believes in him should not perish but have eternal life.

(Spot *out on Area 2, up on Area 1.*)

Actor 6: He gave his son for a purpose. What of the ache, the void, the loss when there is no purpose, when it is unreasonable that your loved one should die?

Narrator 2: Death is always unreasonable. It is not God's will that any should perish but that all should have eternal life through Christ. We live and die according to the evil in this world. But the day is coming when there shall be no more crying, or sighing, or dying, when God shall wipe away every tear.

(SPOT *out on Area 1, up on Area 2.*)

ACTOR 7: I had so many hopes, and dreams, and plans. But they have all come to nothing. I am lonely, a failure.

NARRATOR 1: The moment comes when we stand alone, childless, orphaned, widowed, deserted, our dreams in fragments. We stand alone, stripped of all relationships. We stand alone before God.

(SPOT *out on Area 2, up on Area 1.*)

(SOLO: *"He's the healer of broken hearts," in* NEW SONGS OF INSPIRATION, *No. 8, Benson.*)

NARRATOR 2: Will it really work, or is it just a sentimental song? When the music stops and the night is dark and I'm alone, will those words ring true? When the tears are there, and the aching heart, there is no sweet voice singing then, just the harsh sound of my groans.

NARRATOR 1: That is the time when the song is born. Call upon God. Ask the Holy Spirit to fill your need. Give God a chance to prove his love to you.

(CHOIR: *"Come, Holy Spirit," in* PREPARE YE THE WAY, *Augsburg Publishing House.*)

(ACTORS *come out to center stage area, backs to audience. Face audience on line, then turn back.*)

ACTOR 8: What about inflation? The high cost of living? Expenses, budgets, and making ends meet? The high cost of food?

Narrator 1: You can cut your food bills 14½ percent immediately, instantly! Fast one day in seven.

Actor 9: I love music but the cost of the symphony and the opera is so high, I can't afford it.

Narrator 2: Listen to a bird singing. Listen to the answering chorus at dawn. Listen to the wind in the pines. No charge.

Actor 10: There are so many books I'd like to buy, the latest novels and biographies. But they are so expensive.

Narrator 1: Read the greatest book of all, the Bible. Memorize it. Write it on your heart. No charge.

Actor 11: Works of art are so expensive. I love them but I can't buy them.

Narrator 2: Look at the clouds piling high in sunset splendor, at the branches of a tree etched against pale sky. Watch the slender moon rise. No charge.

Actor 12: I don't know *what* I want! But if I did know, I'm broke and I couldn't afford to buy it.

Narrator 1: Lift your heart in praise to God. No charge.

Actor 1: I want to give presents to those I love, but the prices on everything are so high I can't afford to.

Narrator 2: Go to them and say the most wonderful words of all, "I love you. God loves you." No charge.

ACTOR 2: I have problems and I need someone to help me, someone to talk to, someone who cares about me.

NARRATOR 1: Pray. Claim the promises of God. Live by them. Be a disciple of Christ. No charge. The cost has been paid by the Son of God.

(ORCHESTRA: *Bridge.)*

NARRATOR 1: Women of the past, the present, the future. What of the future? The future is in our hands. (SPOT *on* MOTHERS *with babies in both Acting Areas.)* Each of us holds the future in our hands. Our decisions, our actions, our deeds, will determine the present and the future. Our children, our grandchildren, our great-grandchildren are the future. God said, "He who loves me and keeps my commandments shall be blessed from generation unto generation." Take your future and walk with God.

(CHOIR: *"O Master, let me walk with thee."* MOTHERS *slowly walk away with babies.* SPOTS *fade.)*

NARRATOR 1: We face the future and we see our bridge of hope—the bridge called "Nothing Less." There are bridges made of iron and steel and spans of concrete, seemingly indestructible.

NARRATOR 2: There are bridges of rubber and planks that stretch across hot jungle ponds, bridges of rope and wood stretching across remote mountain ravines.

(During the following narration the Actors *assemble bridge by turning the two platforms at right angles and pushing them together centerstage with ramps on opposite ends.)*

Narrator 1: There are bridges of beauty.

Narrator 2: Bridges that are practical.

Narrator 1: Bridges that are unused, closed off.

Narrator 2: Bridges that fill each day with streaming lines of humanity and machines.

Narrator 1: Bridges that are just for show, arching across a lily pond, used by no one.

Narrator 2: There are bridges in the cities.

Narrator 1: Bridges in the villages.

Narrator 2: Over rushing rivers.

Narrator 1: Over small streams.

Narrator 2: In the country.

Narrator 1: In the desert.

Narrator 2: In the mountains.

Narrator 1: But the most important bridge in the world is the bridge called "Nothing Less."

Narrator 2: Wherever you are you can find that bridge.

Narrator 1: Are you alone on a desert island?

Narrator 2: The bridge is there.

Narrator 1: Are you in a metropolitan maze of frustrating traffic?

Narrator 2: The bridge is there.

Narrator 1: Wherever you are the bridge is there.

Narrator 2: The bridge called "Nothing Less."

Narrator 1: It is built for eternity.

Narrator 2: It is a narrow bridge just wide enough for two.

Narrator 1: Yet wide enough for all who choose to enter there.

Narrator 2: It is safe enough for the most faltering footstep.

Narrator 2: Strong enough for the heaviest load.

Narrator 2: Bright enough to show the way no matter how dark the night.

Narrator 1: The Bridge of Nothing Less.

Narrator 2: It takes you from where you are to where you want to go.

(Choir: *"My hope is built on nothing less than Jesus' blood and righteousness," stanza 1.*)

Narrator 1: Over that bridge called "Nothing Less than Jesus' blood and righteousness" countless souls have crossed.

Narrator 2: Above and beyond wherever we are or whatever we see, we see the Christ, our bridge of hope.

Narrator 1: Rising high over that bridge of hope is the cross of Christ.

Narrator 2: We think of the cross of Christ and we get used to that. *(One tall cross is placed center of bridge.)* We accept it.

Narrator 1: We may even expand it to three crosses at Calvary and we accept that. *(Two smaller crosses are placed left and right of larger cross.)*

Narrator 2: It becomes so familiar—three crosses.

Narrator 1: But there were many more. Oh, there were many more.

Narrator 2: Paul said, "I am crucified with Christ."

Narrator 1: Christ said, "Take up your cross and follow me."

Narrator 2: There are many more crosses than three at Calvary.

Narrator 1: There is a cross for you and me. . . .

Narrator 2: On that Bridge of Nothing Less. . . . than Jesus' blood and righteousness.

(Solo: *"Were you there when they crucified my Lord?"* Actors: *each carries a cross and puts it in place on bridge, and remains in position beside cross.)*

Narrator 1: Reshape us, Lord, reform us, transform us.

Narrator 2: Then may the Holy Spirit fill us and reach out through us and accomplish your miracles of feeding the hungry—

Narrator 1: Clothing the naked.

Narrator 2: Healing the sick.

Narrator 1: Comforting the sorrowing.

Narrator 2: Loving the lonely.

Narrator 1: Giving the water of eternal life to those thirsting for righteousness.

Narrator 2: May our lives be a continual witness of your love. . . .

Narrator 1: That we may bring all we meet. . . .

Narrator 2: Across the Bridge of Nothing Less. . . .

Narrator 1: than Jesus' blood and righteousness. . . .

Narrator 2: Into the glorious day of God's eternal love.

(Solo: *"Reach out and touch,"* in Sing 'N' Celebrate, *Word Music. During the song,* Actors *and* Narrators *come on stage and hold hands. The song is repeated the second time with* Choir *and* Actors *joining in on song. As they sing they move down into audience and invite the entire audience to hold hands.)*

CHRISTMAS MADONNA

A Play in One Act for Five Women

CHARACTERS

Mary

Kate

Donna

Sally

Jean

SETTING

A living room which may be as simple or elaborate as desired. A table and five chairs are necessary as well as a telephone on small table stage left. Table is center stage. A sixth chair is nearby. A sofa and small table may be placed stage right. There are two entrances, one stage right, the other stage left.

PROPS

Christmas gift wrappings, a pile of old Christmas cards, articles of clothing, scissors, quilt pieces to be sewn during the play.

(As play opens, MARY, the hostess, enters from off right, humming and carrying an armful of Christmas wrappings, boxes, scissors, materials for quilts, etc. She puts them on table center. Straightens chairs at table, moves a sixth chair over to table. Goes out right. Phone rings. She enters, carries another box in, crosses over to phone, and awkwardly reaches over to table to put down the other box as she answers.)

MARY *(on phone):* Hello? Oh, hi, Jean—Oh, that's too bad. We'll miss you.— Yes, I know—the Christmas rush. I hate to see it come. Oh, I saw that, too, wasn't it awful? And Don's market, too. Christmas decorations weeks before Halloween! I'll tell the others you can't come, at least I hope there *are* others. Everyone gets so busy now. O.K. I'll see you Sunday. Goodbye. *(Hangs up phone as doorbell rings. She crosses to door and opens it, if there is a door, or else calls "Come in." KATE and DONNA come in, arms loaded with boxes and articles of clothing. Exchange of ad lib greetings.)*

KATE: Sally's right behind us. I got these from the church on the way.

MARY: Jean just called. She can't make it.

DONNA: Oh, wouldn't you know? You can never count on her.

KATE: Well, she does have a lot to do.

DONNA: Don't we all!

MARY: At least she means well. She always seems to *want* to help. We mustn't be too hard on her.

DONNA: But I've got Scripture on my side. It isn't being catty if you can quote Scripture, is it?

KATE: It depends on the Scripture!

DONNA: Well, "It's better to say you can't do something and do it, than to say you will and then don't!" I'm not sure *where* it says that, but I know it does.

MARY: Now, come on, lay off Jean. Let the Christmas spirit prevail. Here, let's start wrapping.

(The three sit down at the table. During the play there is the business of wrapping packages or sewing on quilts or other clothing items. A good chance to get real work done! The women get up at will to get more materials or put completed work in piles. Coffee and cookies may be served if desired.)

KATE: Oh, Mary, you have such lovely gift wrappings. But you always do everything so beautifully.

MARY: I thought we should make the packages as pretty as possible. I know if I were in an orphanage I would want things to be pretty.

KATE: I would too, but I'm very clumsy when it comes to trimming packages. I'm all thumbs. Why don't I do the wrapping and you girls trim?

DONNA: We can do it however it turns out.

(They start wrapping. SALLY knocks and comes in.)

SALLY: Hi! Is the work all done? *(Ad lib greetings.)* I didn't wait for you to open the door. I thought you'd be up to your elbows in ribbon. *(She carries more articles of clothing and wrappings and a box with old Christmas cards in it.)* I brought a bunch of old Christmas cards that I've saved. Thought they'd be pretty on some of the packages.

KATE: That's a good idea.

MARY: Glad you could make it, Sally. Jean phoned that she won't be able to come.

SALLY: Oh, she never does anything she says she's going to.

DONNA: We've already roasted Jean. Who's next?

SALLY: Well, Jim and I are fighting. Want to hear about that?

KATE: Oh, I can give you another subject for discussion. I've really been going round and round with my daughters.

MARY: What's the trouble?

KATE: Their rooms. They simply will not clean up their rooms. How can they be so messy? Where did I go wrong? And Janet wants to change her major and she's a *senior*. And Cathy is in love—again! And they tell me I'm to leave them alone.

DONNA: 'Tis the season to be jolly.

SALLY: That's what I told Jim. It's Christmas, I said, and we're fighting over the Christmas lights. Again.

DONNA: How do you manage to fight over Christmas lights?

SALLY: Well, Jim wanted to be the first one to get them up this year because he said he didn't want me nagging him about it like I do every year. So he got all the lights out of the garage the day before Thanksgiving. Then all I said was I didn't think that we should put them up this year because of the power situation and ecology and things. So he simply blew up and said he could never do anything right and that no matter what he did I found fault or wanted something different. I began to cry, and I said here I had been wanting everything to be beautiful this Christmas, and he said he wanted everything beautiful all the time and not only Christmas. *(There is a short pause.)*

KATE: Christmas!

MARY: I know. I almost hate to see it come. I always know how I want everything to be, and then it never seems to work out quite the way I hoped.

KATE: Same with me. I left my girls in tears. We were fighting. Why? I want to be such a good mother. And suddenly there we were screaming at each other. Is that your idea of a Christian mother?

SALLY: Am I your idea of a Christian wife?

DONNA: I don't think any of us rate ourselves as being the perfect example.

KATE: Well, what's wrong? Here we are, Christian women, and we're supposed to know the answers.

MARY: I don't think knowing the answers is enough. We're supposed to *live* the answers. And there's where the trouble begins. We want to be saints, and we're so human

KATE: Well, I'm human enough—but I sometimes think my daughters are *in*human! They wear such dreadful looking clothes and they never want to wear shoes, always want to go barefoot, and they're late everywhere.

MARY: I know. Sons can be difficult, too. I still can't get Steve to cut his hair or shave off his beard. He looks so—so weird. I try not to be ashamed of his looks, but I just am—and I can't help it. He goes barefoot, too, and in those ragged jeans with patches. And his scraggly beard. Hand me the scissors will you? (*She takes scissors from* DONNA *and cuts ribbon.*) I'd like to use these on Steve! (*They all laugh.*)

KATE: Donna, you're the only one here who doesn't seem to have problems.

DONNA: Oh, I have problems. My problem is *me*. I don't have a husband or children and that leaves me with me. And I get lonely and frightened and critical. You noticed I was the one jumping on Jean because she isn't here. I get bitter—and jealous—and *hate* myself. Yech! (*She makes face.*)

MARY: We're putting the wrappings *on* the packages and taking them *off* of ourselves. True confessions time. Is this what you'd call a "wrap" session? (*Others groan at the pun.*)

SALLY (*holds up Christmas card from pile of cards to be used in trimming*): Look at this card. Mary is holding the baby Jesus. She looks so beautiful, so calm and serene, gentle and wise. The Christmas madonna. *(Hands card to* KATE.*)*

KATE: Oh, it is beautiful. They make such lovely cards.

SALLY: Why can't I be peaceful and gentle and wise, filled with love and perfection like Mary? Instead of fighting with Jim all the time! *(Picks up another card.)* Look at this one: the shepherds and the sheep, everything so beautiful and calm and peaceful. *(Passes the card on.)*

MARY *(reaching over and taking another card)*: Here's one of Mary and Joseph. Mary looks so remote, Joseph so patient and protective.

DONNA *(looking at card* MARY *is holding)*: The wisemen are so noble and dignified. The shepherds so —reverent.

KATE: Here's one with Bethlehem and the star. Bethlehem looks so tranquil and still. That's not the way it's been at our house lately.

SALLY: Everything looks so passive, so unreal. *(Pause.)* Hey! That's it.

KATE: What's it?

SALLY *(examining card)*: Everything looks so *un*real and *un*lifelike. So *un*human. They don't show it like it really was—and is.

DONNA: Sure! The world doesn't look like this now, and it didn't look like this then. Bethlehem didn't look like this, a beautiful perfect little town when Christ was born.

MARY *(getting into the spirit of discovery)*: Of course not! It was hot and dirty and noisy. No plumbing!

KATE: I see what you mean. Since Christ came into the world of man as one of us, he came into a human scene, and if it was human. . . .

SALLY: There had to be trouble, discomfort, pain, and problems.

DONNA: Frustrations and fatigue.

MARY: What was it really like for Mary to be a mother?

KATE: She must have had her problems, too.

SALLY: Of course she did.

DONNA: What was it really like for our Christmas madonna—to leave her home at such at time. . . .

MARY: Leave her family and friends, leave everything that had been prepared for the new baby, and ride a donkey to Bethlehem.

DONNA: They always show her looking so peaceful on that donkey.

KATE: But the donkey undoubtedly stumbled and jogged over the uneven rocky trails.

SALLY: No wonder the time came for her to be delivered!

DONNA: She was probably homesick for her home. How good it must have seemed to her as she remembered how quiet and clean everything was at home.

MARY: When they finally came to that cave back of the inn, the manger so dark and cold and bare. . . .

KATE: The fields outside so rough with rocks and sharp stones.

SALLY: Why Joseph might even have been cross and impatient—like my Jim!

DONNA: He probably didn't get any supper that night with all the noisy crowds around.

MARY: And surely he was worried.

KATE: And how does a worried, hungry man usually act?

SALLY: Maybe Mary might even have nagged Joseph —the way I nag Jim—about how they should have stopped when she first suggested it, there was a much nicer place back there a ways.

DONNA: Since Jesus was born in a human scene, they undoubtedly acted human.

MARY: And how has the conversation been sounding in your kitchen lately?

KATE: You know the answer to that.

SALLY: Did Joseph stay there with Mary?

DONNA: Or did he leave her alone while he took care of that tax business?

KATE: Was Mary alone in the lonely night?

DONNA: With the lonely fears that creep into your soul like spears of ice in the night, the cold, dark, lonely night. How well I know!

MARY: Then once they got settled in that cave, there was no quiet, no chance to rest.

SALLY: There were the sounds of noisy travellers in the inn, late travellers passing on the road all night.

KATE: And all those angels and heavenly hosts flying about, bursting into song at the drop of a star—or halo!

DONNA: Shepherds coming and going, sheep running all over the place.

MARY: What confusion it must have been! No silence or privacy or quiet at all.

SALLY: The silent night we keep singing about—whoever got that idea?

DONNA: That's right! It would be much better to sing "Noisy night, holy night, all is not calm, but all is bright."

(They all join in laughter as doorbell sounds or a knock. MARY crosses to door calling "Come in." JEAN enters. They all ad lib greetings.)

JEAN: I decided to come after all. I felt guilty about not coming after I said I would. It seems I'm always breaking my word.

DONNA: Well, join the party. We've all been having the guilties.

JEAN: I thought you'd all be full of the Christmas spirit!

KATE: Well, we are! The first Christmas spirit.

(They all laugh except JEAN who looks bewildered.)

JEAN: What do you mean?

SALLY: Well, we've been talking about how we fail, and the kind of women we want to be.

DONNA: And how we want Christmas to be but it never seems to be.

MARY: And then Sally showed us a Christmas card.

KATE: And we started talking about how Christmas cards look so beautiful and peaceful and why can't our lives be like that?

SALLY: And then we said that the cards make it looks so beautiful and peaceful and unreal, and that's not how things probably were at all. And we started talking about how things really were.

SALLY: And then Donna said the song shouldn't be "Silent night" at all but "Noisy night"!

JEAN: Hey, I'm glad I came. You sound like you've been having a great time. It surely wasn't a silent night at our house last night. Our baby cried all night and kept us up. That's why I felt so tired this morning that I felt I just couldn't come.

MARY: Oh, that's too bad. But that fits right in with what we've been talking about. Babies do cry. How could things be calm that first Christmas

night? Sleep in heavenly peace? How could anyone sleep at a time like that?

JEAN *(getting into the spirit of it):* With cattle low-
ing in the next stall.

DONNA: You're getting the idea.

JEAN: More heavenly hosts arriving.

KATE: Alleluias ricocheting all over the sky.

JEAN: Why it must have been the noisiest, busiest
night of all eternity.

SALLY: When the Son of God came into the world
of humanity.

DONNA: Sure. And then what happened after that
night? They had to wait around in that cave for
months waiting for the Wise Men to arrive.

MARY: And who said there were three Wise Men?
There might have been four or many more.

KATE: And they had to be fed.

SALLY: And what was there for supper?

JEAN: And all those camels!

(ALL *laugh.*)

DONNA: How did Mary cook and do the dishes?

MARY: They never put any of that on the Christmas
cards.

KATE: Then Joseph started dreaming.

SALLY: So back on that donkey!

Jean: And the long terrible journey down into Egypt.

Donna: Have you been to Egypt?

Mary: No, and I'd love to go. The pictures on the cards look so lovely.

Kate: Always a moonlit path, a star, a palm tree, a benign camel or two.

Sally: Jim and I went to Egypt. We fought all over the place. Have you ridden a camel lately? They're mean! They bite!

Jean: Or a donkey? They bounce!

Donna: There must have been winds and dust storms in that desert.

Mary: And heat and cold and mud.

Kate: Weariness, thirst, and hunger.

Sally: And having to find streams to do all that laundry in.

Jean: Yes, Mary must have had her problems with diapers, just the way I do.

Donna: She had very human, frustrating problems just like us. For that was the point of it all, wasn't it? That Christ should come down into the world of men as men know it—and women.

Mary: Then they had to stay in Egypt. How long? and where?

Kate: And all those flies left over from the plague! Sticky, buzzy, crawly, clinging flies. Ugh!

SALLY: They're *still* there. The flies, I mean. How I hate flies!

JEAN: Did she have enough dishes and blankets and clothes?

DONNA: What food did they have and how did Mary cook it?

MARY: There's no talk about angels helping her with the cooking.

KATE: Then—just when she's gotten things settled in Egypt—there went Joseph with those dreams again.

SALLY: So back on that donkey for the weary way to Nazareth.

JEAN: Then Jesus was a growing boy, filled with eagerness, energy, curiosity. Mary probably had as much trouble keeping track of him as we do our own kids.

DONNA: Maybe he forgot to come in before dark.

MARY: He might even have been late for meals.

KATE: And I wouldn't be a bit surprised if that time in Jerusalem wasn't the first time Mary and Joseph lost track of him.

SALLY: And I suppose he got involved in fights.

JEAN: It would have been a natural thing for all the kids in the neighborhood to pick on him if he started that "No fighting back" business and "turn the other cheek" early in his life.

Donna: Uh-huh! And it would have been complete-ly natural and expected if he brought home every stray cat and dog and sick bird—every lost, lonely little thing that needed love and care in the whole town of Nazareth and beyond.

Kate: My Cathy is always doing that. And I bet he was always giving away his robes and sandals, always finding someone who needed them more than he did. Cathy gave her sweater away just last week—her new pink one that her grandmother sent her.

Mary: Poor Mary! I feel much more like her name-sake now. She must have been distracted and dis-traught most of the time, just like the rest of us.

Sally: Then Jesus was a teen-ager leaving home all the time, not telling Mary where he was going, running around the countryside.

Mary: With that long hair and beard—like my Steve —wearing those funny sandals.

Kate: Or going barefoot.

Sally: Roaming about, not eating well, grabbing an ear of corn here and there.

Jean: Sleeping out on the beaches.

Donna: Getting the best people in town upset.

Jean: Roving about with the most undesirable com-panions.

Donna: People who had sinned and needed help.

Jean: Flaunting all the conventions and traditions.

Kate: Upsetting the authorities.

Jean: Many folks probably called him a rebel, with all his peace talks and disturbing protests down at the synagogue upsetting everyone.

Donna: I suppose we could say that when all's said and done he came to a bad end, according to many of the gossips.

Mary: Yes, our Christmas madonna must have had a real, frustrating, human hard time.

Kate: A time of fears and tears.

Sally: Worry and weariness.

Jean: Trying to bring up the Son of God.

(Moment of silence.)

Donna: You know—suddenly I feel much closer to Mary and the whole set-up of Christmas.

Mary: I don't feel so alone anymore with my problems. The other Mary must have had problems, too.

Kate: And though we've had fun laughing about them, we can be serious too, and realize that God was with her, the same Heavenly father who's with us in our problems today.

Donna: God was with her in her loneliness—just as he has promised to be with me.

Jean: That's right. I'm glad Christmas is coming. It's the celebration of Christ's birthday. And we should stay focused on him, the Savior, and rejoice that the Messiah has come to save his people from their sins.

SALLY: It is the celebration of Christ's birthday, but when you think of it, what a funny celebration it is. It's his birthday, but we get the presents.

JEAN: And we let everyone know very definitely what we want, what model, size and brand.

DONNA: How the cash registers rejoice in rhythm with the Christmas hymns. Any more work for me to do?

MARY: Yes, you can start working on this quilt.

SALLY: But the gift gorging isn't the worst part of it.

JEAN: What do you mean?

SALLY: Every year, out comes the manger scene and the babe in swaddling clothes! On your son's birthday will you say, "Today our son is 33, and here's his baby picture?" Or will you show the latest picture that you have?

JEAN: I see what you mean. On George Washington's birthday, do we drag out his baby picture? Or Abe's?

DONNA: You're right! On Christ's birthday we should rejoice over the risen Lord.

JEAN: Too many people leave Jesus as a baby in the manger all through the year and they fail to see him as the risen Lord.

MARY: Right! So what if a baby was born in Bethlehem 2000 years ago?

KATE: Right! So what? Unless he is the risen Lord.

SALLY: Since Christmas is to celebrate Christ's birthday, let's truly make it his day in remembrance of him and stop worrying about ourselves so much.

JEAN: And we shouldn't make Christmas just one day, but the whole year should be a time of sharing and caring. Not just Christmas. I'm glad I got here in time to help with the gifts for the children's home. And I'll try to come regularly after this. Not just Christmas.

DONNA: Everyday should be a day for giving and living for others.

MARY: I'm getting excited thinking about the Christmas that's coming, a quiet time, a lovely time, a loving time. What difference whether I get the cookies and the fruitcake baked.

KATE: It should be a time of peace and rejoicing over the birth of our Savior, not a time of working in the kitchen.

SALLY: Soft candlelight and the music of Christmas. I'm looking forward to the real Christmas. And I want to make it a special time of loving Jim—and then keep it up through the whole year.

JEAN: On Christmas day we can give our gifts to Christ. We can give him our hearts, our love, our faith, our wills, our lives.

DONNA: We can sing, "Noisy night, holy night, all is not calm, but all is bright. Live in heavenly peace. Live in heavenly peace."

MARY: We can read the story of Bethlehem and Christmas, start out with the baby in the manger, get all excited about the angels.

KATE: Then move from the manger right up to the right hand of God and finish with the angel's words, "You men of Galilee," and Cincinnati, and Chicago and Oskaloosa, Iowa, "Why do you stand gazing up into heaven? This same Jesus who is taken up from you into heaven shall so come in like manner as you have seen him go."

JEAN: Even so, Lord Jesus, come quickly. *(Moment of silence.)*

DONNA: I'm ready for Christmas.

MARY: Just look at how much work we've accomplished.

KATE: The time has passed so quickly.

SALLY: I'm looking forward to our meeting in January.

JEAN: And right on through the year. I'll try never to break my promise again.

MARY: *(starts to gather things up):* Let's take these things over to the church right now.

DONNA: We can sing our new version of "Silent night" for pastor. Come on, let's practice it right now.

ALL: *(gather together and sing):* Noisy night, holy night, all is not calm, but all is bright/Round yon virgin mother and child, holy infant so tender and mild/Live in heavenly peace, live in heavenly peace. *(They laugh and pick up packages and start off.)*

KATE: Oh, it's going to be a wonderful Christmas!

SALLY: I can hardly wait to see Jim and ask him to forgive me and wish him a Merry Christmas.

MARY: Come on, there's lots of giving and living to do.

JEAN: Merry Christmas to all!

DONNA: I wonder how pastor will like our song?

(They all leave. We hear them sing "Noisy night" as they fade off into distance.)

FORWARD IN FAITH

A Reformation Celebration

CHARACTERS

Luther

Inquisitor

2 Narrators

Actors, eight or more

Choir

Drummer

Organist

Trumpeters

ACTORS

Men and women, or all women, who serve as banner bearers, chorus, crowd, council members. There should be an even number, 6-20. Four narrators may be used.

PROPS

Two narrators stand to the right and left of chancel area. Luther uses the regular pulpit. For the opening procession there should be a bright medieval banner for each Actor in the procession to carry. Have fixtures mounted behind railing so the standards can be held and the banners form the bright background for pageant. Actors have tin cans containing coins.

COSTUMES

LUTHER may wear monk's robe and sandals and skull cap or he may be dressed in black. INQUISITOR may be dressed in red costume authentic to period or wear black. All other ACTORS should be dressed in black with red robes to put on during the trial scene. These may be red choir robes or simple red capes donned over the black long-sleeved tops and black slacks.

(Processional is played by Organ. *The* Actors *process down center aisle, each actor carrying a bright medieval banner on a standard.* Actors *are followed by the* Narrators, Inquisitor, *and* Luther *in single file. The* Narrators *take their place behind the* Narrator *stands.* Inquisitor *sits in front pew.* Luther *crosses up and sits in chair behind pulpit.* Actors *go up to chancel and put banners in place and take position across stage.)*

Narrator 1: Every day is reformation, recreation, renewal of the Christian faith. Even as we move forward in reformation, it is right that we look back to one of the great historic moments of Christianity.

*(*Drum *beats slowly as* Actors *move into position.)*

Actors *(softly, gradually increasing volume):* Reformation, Reformation, Reformation, Reformation!

Narrator 1: What reformation?

Actors: The Protestant Reformation.

Narrator 2: Who protested?

Actors: Martin Luther—and many others.

Narrator 1: Why? What was the point?

Actors: They wanted more freedom.

Narrator 2: People always want more freedom. Freedom for what?

Actors: To find their way to God.

Narrator 1: And did they find their way?

Actors: Yes!

Narrator 2: And everyone . . .

Narrator 1: Everywhere . . .

Narrator 2: In each century . . .

Narrator 1: Each year . . .

Narrator 2: Each day . . .

Narrator 1: Must still continue in his search for God.

Narrator 2: How did it all begin?

Actors: It began with the blow of a hammer.

Narrator 2: The hammer held in the hand of Martin Luther.

Narrator 1: It began with the sound of jingling coins.

(Actors *hold out tin cans with coins in them which they shake as they circle about stage.*)

Actors: As soon as the coin in the coffer rings, the soul from purgatory springs. As soon as the coin in the coffer rings, the soul from purgatory springs. Indulgences! Indulgences! Buy your indulgences from Tetzel! Help build St. Peter's in Rome! (*Return to their places on stage.*)

Narrator 1: John Tetzel, a Dominican friar and expert salesman of indulgences, came to Wittenberg in Central Germany to sell indulgences which would grant complete remission of penalties in this world and the next to all who would make a suitable contribution to the building fund of St. Peter's Church in Rome.

Narrator 2: The same remission of penalties would be granted to the souls in purgatory if the living would make the contribution for them. This was the detonator for the Ninety-five Theses of Martin Luther. They were the result of years of study, soul searching, seeking, and sincere prayer on the part of Martin Luther.

Narrator 1: Who was Martin Luther?

Narrator 2: Who was this man who struck the hammer blow on October 31, 1517?

Actors (*softly chanting*): Martin Luther, Martin Luther, Martin Luther, Martin Luther . . . protested!

Narrator 1: What did he protest?

Actors: He protested against the darkness.

Narrator 2: Why?

Actors: He saw light in the darkness and he wanted that light to shine to all people.

Narrator 1: What was that light?

Actors: The light was Christ.

Narrator 2: Who was Martin Luther?

Actors: Martin Luther was a great wind blowing through the mighty forest of men. He was the lightning of God against a night sky of sin, an instrument in the hand of God, and thunder in the still mountains of men's souls. (Trumpet *sounds*.) He was a trumpet, a trumpet giving a battle cry.

Narrator 1: Martin Luther was a man, a very human, down-to-earth man, often sick, frightened, lonely. He was brave and had courage to speak out for what he believed, but he was an ordinary man.

ACTORS: An ordinary man? But what is ordinary? If sunlight is ordinary, if a split atom is ordinary, if the air we breathe is ordinary, why, yes, Luther was an ordinary man.

NARRATOR 2: Luther was an ordinary man who dared to be used by God, who dared to be true to what he believed, the truth revealed by God in his word.

ACTORS: He began to read the Bible that was chained to the monastery wall.

NARRATOR 1: Luther was in torment. Where could he find peace?

ACTORS: He was crushed beneath the burden of mortality.

NARRATOR 2: Where was salvation?

ACTORS: He felt damned by the awful justice of God.

NARRATOR 1: And suddenly one day, or one night . . .

ACTORS: Like a blazing shaft of red glory piercing the monastic gloom . . .

NARRATOR 2: Like a crashing crescendo of mighty thunder . . .

ACTORS: Like the slender, silver shaft of faith that explodes the universe . . .

NARRATOR 1: He read these words: "The just shall live by faith."

Actors (*repeating softly*): "The just shall live by faith."

Narrator 2: There was his answer. There was his peace.

Actors: There was forgiveness and truth.

Narrator 1: This was the tiny beginning.

Actors: The shaft of light in his solitary gloom. The splitting of the atom of faith. Booom!

Narrator 2: He began to study more and more. He ate the Scriptures like bread—like manna. And as he studied he began to ask questions.

Actors: Questions that buzzed like bees, questions that pricked at his heart, questions that stung his mind.

Narrator 1: How deep is the heart of a man? How far into space can a man's thoughts go? Martin Luther tried to find out.

Actors: The questions built up like a tidal wave: higher, higher, higher, higher!

Narrator 2: Until the wave swept him down to the very door of the great cathedral of Wittenberg.

Actors: Down through the night-filled street he went, under the dawn-filling sky he went, up to the door, the great thick door and he hammered there his questions.

(Slow heavy beats of the drum like the pounding of a hammer. Luther goes up into pulpit. Drum beats a single beat to introduce each thesis and beats at the conclusion of each one.)

ACTORS: Number twenty. *(Drum beat.)*

LUTHER: The pope by his plenary remission of all penalties does not mean the remission of all penalties absolutely—but only those imposed by himself. *(Drum beat.)*

ACTORS: Twenty-one. *(Drum beat.)*

LUTHER: Therefore those preachers of indulgences are in error who allege that through the indulgence a man is freed from every penalty. *(Drum beat.)*

ACTORS: Twenty-two. *(Drum beat.)*

LUTHER: For he remits to souls in purgatory no penalty which they had been bound, according to the canons, to pay in this life. *(Drum.)*

ACTORS: Twenty-three. *(Drum.)*

LUTHER: If any complete remission of penalties can be given to anyone, it is sure that it can be given only to the most perfect, that is, to very few. *(Drum.)*

ACTORS: Twenty-four. *(Drum.)*

LUTHER: And therefore it follows that the greater part of the people is deceived by this indiscriminate and liberal promising of freedom from penalty. *(Looks up from the scroll from which he has been reading.)* The just shall live by *faith* in Jesus Christ. Good works are the outward demonstration of that faith. Salvation is not purchased by good works or indulgences. *(Drum.)*

ACTORS: Forty-three. *(Drum.)*

Luther *(reading):* Christians are to be taught that to give to the poor or to lend to the needy is a better work than the purchase of pardons. *(Looking up from scroll.)* Men are saved by faith alone in the sacrifice of Jesus Christ.

(Drum beats slowly as Luther steps down from pulpit and Actors move down to sit in front pews.)

Choir: *Anthem or hymn.*

Narrator 1: And so the Protestant Reformation was born. It came in the autumn of the Middle Ages, in a time of great religious ferment. Many religious leaders were troubled over the need for reforms in religious matters. Men everywhere were seeking spiritual salvation, renewal, the better world of Christian promise.

Narrator 2: Martin Luther, an instrument in God's hand, fitted most significantly into this time in history. The time, the historical setting, and the impact of other troubled spiritual leaders contributed to the Reformation. Still, it is to this one man that history points as the beginning, the detonator of the spiritual explosion that followed.

Narrator 1: Martin Luther, born November 10, 1483, died in 1546: a life span of 63 years. The Protestant Reformation, born in 1517 is still growing. It is a continuing reformation. We are still seeking, still searching out God's will, still moving forward in faith. Reformation, recreation, renewal, reaffirmation.

Narrator 2: 1517: one Luther.

LUTHER *(in pulpit):* Do not call yourselves Luther-ans! Call yourselves—Evangelicals. Do not look to me. Every man should look to Christ. Follow *him. (Leaves pulpit.)*

NARRATOR 1: But the name Luther remained. First a term of derision. Today, a banner flung high, a banner of faith over more than seventy million Lutherans.

NARRATOR 2: Even more than this: the seeds for the entire Protestant Reformation were sown, seeds that have increased to number over 230 million Protestants.

NARRATOR 1: It was the beginning and it is the continuing in a forward movement of faith of all Christians of the world, Christians everywhere pressing forward in life, new life, a renewal of faith and obedience to God's Word, God's Son, God's Spirit, God's will.

CHOIR: *Hymn or anthem.*

NARRATOR 1: Martin Luther's questions could not go unanswered. They spread beyond the university, and a clamour arose in every corner of Europe. Luther was challenged, chastised, excommunicated.

NARRATOR 2: His reforms were based on two great principles. The first was the sole authority of the Scriptures. He maintained that the Holy Spirit speaks only through the Word of God, and only that truth can rightly claim to be the word of God which is derived from the canonical Scriptures.

Narrator 1: The second principle was that of love. In making reforms, consideration must be given to the effect they will have on other men. Education in Christian truths must necessarily precede complete reformation in church practice. Respect for constituted authority in all things that do not immediately concern the soul's salvation was ingrained in his nature. The powers that be are ordained of God.

Narrator 2: In 1521 the Holy Roman Emperor, Charles V, called a meeting of all the princes and rulers in Europe to meet in the great, gloomy cathedral in Worms. There Luther was to be questioned, tried, judged, and banned from the empire. The night before, Luther was ill and frightened almost to death. But on the day of the questioning, Luther arrived in a cart, playing a flute on the way. As the city where the meeting was to be held came into view, he stood up in the cart and began to sing a song he had composed just two days before.

(Soloist *sings first stanza of "A mighty fortress."* Actors *wearing red capes slowly move up on platform forming an aisle. At conclusion of song,* Inquisitor, *moves up aisle and turns to face audience. Fanfare of* Trumpets.)

Inquisitor: Martin Luther! Heretic! Fanatic! Rebel! Bring him here before the council.

(Actors *take position of council.* Luther *moves slowly up to pulpit and stands quietly facing* Inquisitor.)

INQUISITOR: O Lord! Arise and judge thy cause. A wild boar has invaded thy vineyard. *(Turns and points to* LUTHER.*)* You, Martin Luther, are that wild boar!

LUTHER *(speaks quietly, soberly, carefully):* Then may the Lamb of God deal with me.

INQUISITOR: You burned the decree issued by the pope and in that burning, you have started a fire that is raging across the continent. You must put out that fire today.

LUTHER: If that fire is not of God's will, surely he will put it out with the water of the Holy Spirit.

INQUISITOR: Must you blaspheme here?

LUTHER: Is it blasphemy to seek God's will?

INQUISITOR: How dare you set yourself up with such authority! Who are you to challenge the church? Would you be so kind as to tell this assembly?

LUTHER: I am Martin Luther, 38 years of age, son of a Saxon miner, loyal and devout servant of the church.

INQUISITOR *(with derision):* Yes! Your loyalty and devotion have brought you here! What delusion brought you into the church? Was it your parents' dream? Was it your boyhood fantasy?

LUTHER: No, my parents opposed it. Especially my father. I had planned to go into law until I reached the age of 22. Then one summer afternoon . . . *(he pauses).*

INQUISITOR: Yes? What changed your course from law?

LUTHER: I was on my way to Stotternheim. A sudden summer storm swept down upon me. A bolt of lightning came crashing out of the heavens and struck me to the ground. I cried out in my terror "St. Anne, help me and I will become a monk." And so I did.

INQUISITOR: Why did you call upon St. Anne?

LUTHER: She is the patron saint of miners, and my father is a miner.

INQUISITOR: So, out of one storm into another! You have been denounced as a man teaching dangerous doctrines. The pope has demanded that you recant your views on pain of excommunication. What conceit, what devil of pride, what disobedience has led you to the precipice?

LUTHER: I have been an obedient monk. I have tried in all ways to be a faithful child of God.

INQUISITOR: Have you always devoutly kept the rules of your order?

LUTHER: I have kept the rules so strictly that if ever a monk got to heaven by his sheer monkery it was I. If I had kept on any longer with my prayers and vigils, my fastings and whippings, I should have killed myself surely.

INQUISITOR: So you admit human frailty and weakness?

LUTHER: I see myself as a weak, mortal sinner. Don't you?

Inquisitor (*in rage*): I am not on trial here!

Luther: Every child of God is always on trial. Always and forever seeking to find God's truth, his will.

Inquisitor: Let us not lose ourselves in generalities. We are here for one purpose: to try you and no one else. Why were you not satisfied with your penances? What self-seeking pride in you—

Luther: No! No! It was a profound sense of my own sinfulness and of God's unutterable majesty that drove me to my despair. I slept without a blanket in the winter winds. I fasted for three days and more, always trying to humiliate self.

Inquisitor: Ah! Perhaps, then, it was when you began to serve in the church that pride overtook you.

Luther: No, not then, not ever—I say humbly before God. When I said my first mass, I was utterly stupefied and terror stricken. I thought, who am I that I should lift up my eyes or raise my hands to the divine majesty? For I am dust and ashes and full of sin, and I am speaking to the living, eternal, and true God.

Inquisitor: This continual humility and self-abasement! All the emphasis on self, self, self!

Luther: No, I was sick of self. There was a great gap between my God and me. Nothing I could do could bridge this great gulf. No one could still my conviction that I was a miserable, doomed sinner.

Inquisitor: Did you feel that you loved God so much more than any one else did?

Luther: No! I almost came to the place where I hated God instead of loving him. I trembled at the thought of his terrible justice! And then—

Inquisitor: Yes? And then?

Luther: When I was appointed to the faculty at Wittenberg University to lecture in biblical studies, I became the student. The theme that kept recurring was righteousness—righteousness by faith. Romans, the first chapter, sixteenth and seventeenth verses. They seemed to be burned as if by fire in my brain—"For I am not ashamed of the gospel: it is the power of God for salvation to every one who has faith, to the Jew first and also to the Greek. For in it the righteousness of God is revealed through faith for faith; as it is written, "The just shall live by faith."

Inquisitor: Do you think that you are the only one to read those words, the only one who knows their meaning?

Luther: No. When I visited Rome, I started to climb the holy stairs on my knees. I got halfway up the stairs and that verse thundered in my brain. "The just shall live by faith." I got up off my knees and walked down the stairs. "The just shall live by faith," not by climbing stairs on their knees!

(*Reaction from the* Council.)

Inquisitor: You will be burned at the stake before you're through! You are too presumptuous! Have you already made yourself a saint?

LUTHER: May God in his mercy preserve me from a church in which there are none but saints. I desire to dwell with the humble, the feeble, the sick, who know and feel their sins and who groan and cry continually to God from the bottom of their hearts to obtain his consolation and support.

INQUISITOR: Is there no way to stop you? Did you think you were the first and only one to discover this truth?

LUTHER: I was discovering it for myself for the first time. Truth must always be a personal revelation. Universal truth means nothing unless it is first realized in the individual heart.

INQUISITOR: Yes, yes, yes. Must you persist in preach- to us? Just what was this personal revelation, this truth that *you* discovered?

LUTHER: Night and day I pondered, until I saw the connection between the justice of God and the statement that the just shall live by faith in the gospel of Christ. For it is the power of God unto salvation. Then I grasped that the justice of God is that righteousness of Christ by which, through grace and sheer mercy, God justifies us. Thereupon I felt myself to be reborn and to have gone through open doors into paradise.

INQUISITOR: There is no fault in that. *(Pauses. Raises voice and points to* LUTHER.*)* But it is in the conclusions that you have drawn that you are damning your soul—and the souls of your followers. *(Reaction from* COUNCIL.*)* Have you said that man does not need to confess to a priest?

LUTHER: I said that if faith saves, man does not need
mediators between him and the almighty.

COUNCIL *(ad lib):* Heresy!

LUTHER: If this conclusion damns my soul, then
surely the soul of the Apostle Paul is damned. For
the Apostle Paul said to Timothy, second chapter,
fifth verse, "There is one God and one mediator
between God and men, the man Christ Jesus, who
gave himself as ransom for all."

INQUISITOR: You go too far!

LUTHER: Show me my error by the Scriptures, then,
I beg of you. Prove me my error by using God's
word. The theology of indulgences has been per-
verted. Indulgences cannot free us from guilt.
They have no influence upon purgatory. And they
are harmful because they are misunderstood and
give false confidence and false security to the pur-
chaser.

INQUISITOR *(pointing at* LUTHER*)*: By decree of the
council, anyone who criticizes indulgences is guilty
of heresy.

COUNCIL: Heretic!

LUTHER: A council may sometimes err! *(Reaction
from* COUNCIL.*)* Neither the church nor the pope
can establish articles of faith. These must come
from Scripture. Faith comes by hearing the word
of God. We must search the Scriptures, study
them, preach and teach God's word.

INQUISITOR: Have you said that every man is his own
priest?

LUTHER: Our Baptism consecrates us all without exception and makes us all priests. There is a priesthood of all believers. Man serves God best in his daily existence. If a man makes shoes, let him make even better shoes because he is a Christian.

INQUISITOR *(paces the floor):* Do you dare to translate the Scriptures?

LUTHER: Men everywhere must read God's word and in his own language. I am going to translate the Bible into German so that each man may read the teaching of the Holy Spirit.

INQUISITOR *(pacing, and then whirling on LUTHER):* Are you preaching against celibacy for monks and nuns?

LUTHER *(after a pause):* Let each follow his own preference whether or not to marry. If God has not forbidden marriage, no man should or may do so.

INQUISITOR *(shouting):* Are you setting yourself above the pope himself?

LUTHER I have no such intention. The pope is servant of servants, and more than all other men he is in a most miserable and dangerous position. He should not be deceived by those who pretend that he is lord of the world. They err who exalt him above a council and the church universal.

INQUISITOR: Is there no end to your audacity? Do you want to divide Christianity?

LUTHER: No! I only want the church of God to be strengthened.

INQUISITOR: If you shatter unity, how can you strengthen it?

COUNCIL: Huss! Huss! You are a follower of Huss!

LUTHER: Huss preached that we must confess our sins to Christ and that we cannot pay our way to heaven. He said that heaven is a gift of God. In that I am not ashamed to be compared to Huss.

COUNCIL: Burn him! No! He speaks the truth! Hussite! Burn him!

INQUISITOR: There is no way to reason with you, Martin Luther. There are some twenty or more books that you have written. Are you willing to admit that anything you have written in these books is wrong?

LUTHER: I wrote what I believed with all my heart to be true. If I admit anything I have written is wrong, then I must take back everything I have written.

INQUISITOR: Then you must take back everything.

LUTHER: If I took back everything written in these books, I should be taking back some truths and facts that are believed by you and the church and every true child of God. How can you ask me to take back everything I have written? Show me where I have made a mistake. Show me by the word of God where I have erred, and I shall be the first one to burn them in the fire.

INQUISITOR (after a pause, very deliberately): Martin Luther, will you or will you not recant? Will you or will you not take back what you have spoken or written? Will you or will you not submit to the authority of the council?

LUTHER (*after a pause, with great deliberation, great conviction*): Unless I am convinced by the Holy Scriptures, I neither can nor will take back anything. My conscience is captive to the Word of God. I will not recant. For to go against conscience is neither honest nor safe. Here I stand! I cannot do otherwise. God help me. Amen.

(COUNCIL *forms aisle for two men to leave stage and then follows them off.* DRUM *beats slowly as they exit.*)

CHOIR: *Hymn or anthem.*

NARRATOR 1: "My conscience is captive to the Word of God." These words of Luther have echoed down to us through the years in a march of faith that has spread throughout the world: to Germany, Norway, Sweden, Denmark, Finland, England, Holland, America, Africa—to every continent and island of the world.

NARRATOR 2: The seal that is used to stand as a symbol of the Lutheran Church is the seal that Martin Luther devised while he was a professor at Wittenberg. He declared that this seal was an expression of his theology. In a letter written to his friend, Herr Spengler, town clerk of Nuremberg, Luther explains the meaning of his seal.

LUTHER (*in pulpit reading*): Dear Herr Spengler: You have asked me the meaning of my seal. The first thing expressed in my seal is a cross, black, within the heart, to put me in mind that faith in Christ saves us. "For with the heart man believes unto righteousness." Now, although the cross is black, mortified, and intended to cause pain, yet it does not change the color of the heart, does not destroy nature, that is, does not kill, but keeps alive. "For the just shall live by faith—by faith in the Saviour." This heart is fixed upon the center of a white rose to show that faith causes joy, consolation, and peace. The rose is white, not red, because white is the ideal color of all angels and blessed spirits. This rose, moreover, is fixed in a sky-colored ground, to denote that such joy of faith in the Spirit is but an earnest and beginning of heavenly joy to come, as anticipated and held by hope, though not yet revealed. And around this ground-base is a golden ring to signify that such bliss in heaven is endless, and more precious than all joys and treasures, since gold is the best and most precious metal. Christ, our dear Lord, will give grace unto eternal life. Amen *(exits from pulpit).*

NARRATOR 1: The seal designed by Luther has been the continuing symbol of the church's work. Luther's work was varied and prodigious: preaching, teaching, writing, composing hymns, catechisms and orders of worship. He also established the first Protestant parsonage. Convinced that it was God's will that he marry, Martin Luther married Kathcrine von Bora, who had been a nun in the convent at Nimbschen.

NARRATOR 2: Luther was 42, Katherine 29 when they were married. Katherine had been out of the convent for five years and had turned down several offers of marriage. After much prayer, Martin

Luther asked her to be his wife. They were married at five o'clock in the afternoon on June 13 in the year 1525. A public ceremony was held on the twenty-seventh of June. Luther prayed, "God grant me grace to rule my wife and household in thy fear. Give me wisdom and strength. Amen."

NARRATOR 1: Luther called Katherine, "My lord Kate" and "Katie my rib." They had six children. Descendants from these children are living today. Family devotions were held regularly in the home, and Luther had a close relationship with his children. He told them, "Children, read your Bible. Listen eagerly whenever anyone reads it to you. I was twenty years old before I had ever seen the Bible."

NARRATOR 2: Luther continued to teach at the University of Wittenberg until his death. He said to Kate just before he died, "You're a wonderful wife, my Lord Kate, and I love you with my whole heart and do not want to leave you, but I truly want the Lord Jesus to remove my soul into his care. I am ready to go. I have lived out and finished the course assigned to me by God." He died at the age of 63 in Eisleben on February 18, 1546.

NARRATOR 1: Luther's words of his great conviction at his moment of truth ring down to us through the years. "Unless I am convinced by the Holy Scriptures, I neither can nor will take back anything. My conscience is captive to the Word of God. I will not recant, for to go against conscience is neither honest nor safe. Here I stand. I cannot do otherwise. God help me. Amen."

Narrator 2: "Here I stand." These words ring out through the centuries of Reformation history, and a mighty echo swells up from us today. Here we stand, our conscience captive to the word of God. "The just shall live by faith in the grace of Jesus Christ, son of the living God, our Savior."

Narrator 1: We all join together in the unity of the continuing reformation: Life, new life, in Christ. The daily renewal of Christian faith, a daily commitment to the will of God. Even as Martin Luther was an instrument in the hand of God, let each of us yield ourselves anew to God's will. As we draw closer to God through faith in Jesus Christ, we draw closer to each other in the unity of faith.

Narrator 2: Luther said that all Christian laymen are in the priesthood of believers. Man serves God best in his daily existence. Our baptism consecrates us all without exception and makes us priests. Now, everyone, whatever the congregation or denomination is invited to stand to express faith in Jesus Christ our Lord and to repeat the Apostles' Creed as a witness to our faith.

Congregation (rises): I believe in God the Father almighty, Maker of heaven and earth. And in Jesus Christ his only son, our Lord; who was conceived by the Holy Ghost, born of the virgin Mary, suffered under Pontius Pilate, was crucified, dead, and buried; he descended into hell; the third day he rose again from the dead; he ascended into heaven and sitteth on the right hand of God the Father Almighty; from thence he shall come to judge the quick and the dead. I believe in the Holy Ghost; the holy Christian church, the communion of saints; the forgiveness of sins; the resurrection of the body; and the life everlasting. Amen.

Our Father which art in heaven. Hallowed be thy name. Thy kingdom come. Thy will be done on earth as it is in heaven. Give us this day our daily bread. And forgive us our trespasses, as we forgive those who trespass against us. And lead us not into temptation. But deliver us from evil. For thine is the kingdom and the power and the glory, forever and ever. Amen.

CHOIR: *"Sevenfold Amen."*

NARRATOR 1: Now from our standing position we will move out and go forward in faith, moving ahead in the work to be done, reaching forth unto those things which are before. We will press toward the mark for the prize of the high calling of God in Christ Jesus.

NARRATOR 2: We will live out our faith in our homes, in our schools, in our churches, in our work, to our neighbors, wherever we may be, whatever we do, being careful for nothing but in everything by prayer and supplication with thanksgiving letting our requests be made known unto God.

NARRATOR 1: Finally, whatever is true, whatever is honorable, whatever is just, whatever is pure, whatever is lovely, whatever is gracious, if there is any excellence, if there is anything worthy of praise, think about these things. What you have learned and received and heard and seen in me do; and the God of peace will be with you.

Narrator 2: We can do all things through Christ who strengthens us. The peace of God which passes all understanding shall keep your hearts and minds through Christ Jesus. The grace of our Lord Jesus Christ be with us all as we go forward in faith.

(Choir *sings* "A mighty fortress is our God" *with congregation.* Actors *process down the aisle, followed by the two* Narrators, *then the* Inquisitor *and finally* Luther.)